Hanukkah!

Written by Roni Schotter ◆ Illustrated by Marylin Hafner

Little, Brown and Company

Boston ◆ Toronto ◆ London

For the grandfathers and the grandmothers —
Big Al and Harvey, Mimi and Sara, and, of course, Edna.
R. S.

In memory of my grandfather, Stephen.
M. H.

Text copyright © 1990 by Roni Schotter
Illustrations copyright © 1990 by Marylin Hafner

First edition

Library of Congress Cataloging-in-Publication Data

Schotter, Roni.
    Hanukkah! / written by Roni Schotter; illustrated by Marylin
Hafner.
        p.   cm.
    Summary: Describes the meaning and traditions of Hanukkah as five
children and their family celebrate the holiday.
    ISBN 0-316-77466-9
    1. Hanukkah — Juvenile literature.   [1. Hanukkah.]   I. Hafner,
Marylin, ill.   II. Title.
BM695.H3S38   1989
296.4'35 — dc19   88-28426
                                                                            CIP
                                                                            AC

10   9   8   7   6   5   4   3   2   1

WOR

Joy Street Books are published
by Little, Brown and Company (Inc.)

In darkest December
Night steals in early
And whisks away the light.

But warm inside,
Mama, Papa, and Grandma Rose
Light the sun.

While Nora and Dan,
Ruthie and Sam
Sing a song
That is a prayer.

"Birthday!" Moe points and drops his bottle. "Hot!"
"No, Hanukkah," Sam says, "Say 'Hanukkah,' Moe."
"Abadah, Moe," Moe says. "Abadah!" and drools on Sam's hand.

"Come on," Nora whispers to the others.
And, while the candles burn bright,
Five small children slip out of sight.

Nora and Dan, in the kitchen,
Fry some batter.
Flip, flap here.
Flip, flop there.
Potato pancakes in the air.
Latkes flying everywhere.

Ruthie, in the bedroom,
Mixes some paint.
A drop of blue,
A drop of red,
A drop of purple
On Rabbit's head.

While off in a corner, tucked away,
Sam shapes a dreydel of clay.

"Top!" Moe shouts, spinning round and round.

"Yes, dreydel," Sam says. "For Hanukkah. Say 'Hanukkah,' Moe."

"Anoohah, Moe," Moe says. "Anoohah!" and drools on Sam's foot.

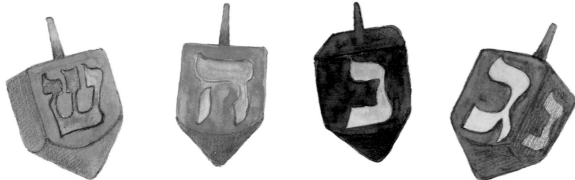

Then . . .
One by one
Their gifts in hand,
The children gather
Round.

Grandma carries her favorite dish,
Pot roast, warm, and brown, and rich.
Papa brings his salad, cool and crisp,
And Mama, her applesauce.
    "Dee-licious!" Moe says.

"The latkes have landed! The latkes have landed!"
Sam shouts, holding out his plate.

Moe grabs five, unable to wait.

And, as the Hanukkah candles
Lean head to head,
So does the family . . .
"Ohhh!"   "Ahhh!"   "Ummm!"
"Yummm!"   "Burp!"

But wait . . . there's more.
There's no escape.
It's Grandma's famous lemon cake!

And cookies,
And candy,
And fruit,
And nuts,
And now *that's all.*
Enough's enough!

Time for presents
Or what's a party?
For songs . . .
For dances . . .

And one thing more . . .

Love!
Light!
Hanukkah!

"Say 'Hanukkah,' Moe," Sam says. "Come on, Moe.
Say, 'Hanukkah'!"

"Anoo . . ." Moe gurgles. "Nanoo . . ." Moe drools.
"Hanoo . . ." Moe giggles. "Hanu-*kkah!*"
Moe shouts and hugs Sam. "Hanukkah!"

And, as the candles burn low and lose their light,
Eight sleepy people say, "GOOD NIGHT."

The Story of Hanukkah
The Festival of Light and Dedication

For more than two thousand years, the old and beautiful holiday of Hanukkah has been celebrated by Jewish people for eight days each December. Hanukkah recalls a time long ago when the Jewish people, led by Judah Maccabee, fought a king named Antiochus for the right to worship their one God, instead of the many gods of the Greek religion. When the Jews won the battle, they cleared away the statues of the Greek gods and rededicated their Temple to one God. Then they celebrated for eight days.

According to legend, Judah Maccabee searched for some pure oil to light the Temple menorah, but found only enough to last one day. But then a miracle occurred: the oil burned for eight whole days. That miracle of lasting light has come to symbolize the meaning of Hanukkah — a celebration of the freedom and determination of Jewish people to practice their religious beliefs freely.

Some Hanukkah Words and What They Mean

 **Dreydel** ✴ A spinning top with four sides, each side with the first letter of one of the four Hebrew words *Nes Gadol Haya Sham,* which mean "A great miracle happened there." The dreydel game is played by putting nuts, candy, or Hanukkah *gelt* (money) into a pile at the center of the floor. Each player spins the dreydel. If it lands on the Hebrew letter *Nun,* the player takes nothing from the pile. If it lands on *Gimel,* the player takes everything. If it lands on *Hey,* the player takes half, if on *Shin,* the player adds something to the pile.

 **Latkes** ✴ A traditional holiday dish of potato pancakes fried in oil.

 **Menorah** ✴ A candle holder or oil lamp with nine branches. At sundown on the first night of the holiday, the shamash, or helper candle, is lit and then used to light the first candle. On the second night, the shamash is used to light two candles. On the third night, it lights three, and so on, until the eighth and final night of the holiday when all the candles are lit.

 **Shamash** ✴ The helper candle, which stands apart from the other menorah candles.

Say "Hanukkah," everyone:

Say *Han* as if it rhymed with the name *Don.*
Say *u* as if it rhymed with the word *zoo.*
Say *kah* as if it rhymed with the words *ma* or *pa.*
Hanukkah!